Copyright Notices

Copyright 2017 Stella Singles LLC

All rights reserved. Any unauthorized transfer of license, use, sharing, reproduction or distribution of these materials by any means electronic, mechanical, or otherwise is prohibited. No portion of these materials may be reproduced in any manner whatsoever without the express written consent of the publishers.

Published under the copyright laws of the Library Of Congress Of The United States Of America by Stella Singles LLC.

Disclaimer

This book and the items it distributes are for entertainment purposes only and individual results may vary. We make absolutely no guarantees, expressed or implied, that by following the advice in this guide you will achieve any results. Results will primarily depend on your personal situation, how you apply the strategies and how much experience you have. If you need professional help, please contact a therapist or a medical practitioner specializing in the field of your issue.

ISBN: 9781521835746

More dating & relationship books by Stella:

Read Her Signs: An Essential Guide To Understanding Women And Never Getting Rejected Again

Flirt Her Up: Learn The Secret Language of Love and Start Connecting With Women Like a Pro

The Road To Confidence: Learn to Conquer Your Fears, Build Self-Confidence and Enjoy Long-Lasting Dating Success

WHAT WOMEN REALLY LIKE IN A MAN

45 Dating Tips on How to Capture a Woman's Heart, Make Her Fall in Love with You (For Good), and Never Want to Leave You!

By Stella Belmar

http://www.StellaDatingCoach.com
http://www.StellaSingles.com

Table of Contents

INTRODUCTION 1

CHAPTER 1. PERSONALITY TRAITS 7

   1. Self Confidence, Not Arrogance 7

   2. Leadership, Not Control 8

   3. Be Funny and Witty 10

   4. Know What You Want 11

   5. Call, Call, Call (or Consistency) 12

   6. Be a Gentleman 14

   7. Be Honest 15

   8. Fight Your Ego 17

   9. Be Generous 18

   10. Be A Good Listener 20

   11. Be Compassionate 21

   12. Be Social 22

   13. Respect Women 23

   14. Don't Constantly Talk About Yourself 24

   15. Dress Nice and Be Clean 24

   16. Don't be a Clean Freak 25

CHAPTER 2. EMOTIONAL TRIGGERS 27

   17. Create Magic 28

   18. Be Passionate 30

19. Out Of Control 32

20. Vulnerability 33

21. Charm/Gallantry 34

22. Physical Touch 35

23. Decisiveness 37

CHAPTER 3. ACTIONS THAT WILL GET YOU NOTICED 39

24. Open Doors 39

25. Bring Flowers 39

26. Send Little Gifts 40

27. Say "Thank You"/Texting 40

28. Say "Hi" 42

29. Pick Her Up 42

30. Be a Handyman 43

31. Be Creative 44

32. Surprise Her 45

33. Show Her You Care About Her Pets 46

34. Show Interest In Her Life 46

35. Wish Her Goodnight and Sweet Dreams 46

36. Helping Without Expectation of Reciprocation 47

37. Emotions 48

38. Embrace Her Hobby 48

39. Bring Her To/From The Airport 49

40. Help Her Draft Her Resume/Work Paper 50

41. Use Romantic Words 50

42. Cook Her Dinner 51

43. Play a Game 51

44. Discuss Topics of Interest 52

45. Travel 52

CHAPTER 4. WHY DATING CAN BE SO COMPLEX 55

CHAPTER 5. MYTHS ABOUT WOMEN 57

CONCLUSION 61

Please Leave A Review 63

Your Free Gift

As a thank you for purchasing this guide and to give you even more information and examples on what women really like, I've included some great bonus material for you. It's a series of audio recordings where I expand on what's covered in this book, give extra examples as well as reveal some secrets on what kind of mistakes to avoid with women.

You will receive 3 audios and there will also be a surprise gift at the end.

Please go to this link to receive your free gift now:

http://stelladatingcoach.com/audio-series-bonus/

INTRODUCTION

Throughout history, men have viewed women with enigma and intrigue, and with good reason. After all, women are very different from men. Beautiful and special as they may be, a mystery they remain.

So, it is no surprise that men often feel confused or overwhelmed when it comes to actually dating a woman they are interested in.

You may be one of these men. Whether you are new to dating or just trying to polish your skills, this book is for you. Maybe you've just come out of a long relationship or maybe you just want to finally stop playing the field and settle down. Regardless, this book will provide the answers you've been looking for. It will show you what makes one man really stand apart from the rest.

While some of these concepts can be applied to casual relationships, the focus of this book is serious dating. If you are interested in being that special man, in standing out from the crowd, in having that special girl notice you and stay with you, keep reading. If you're full of good intentions, but maybe short on ideas, this book is for you. For those out there who feel they already have a good grasp on the whole dating process, perhaps you may be in need of some fresh inspiration. Regardless of your personal situation or back-story, the information in this book can be a great asset when it comes to understanding women.

Let's face it: the female world can seem a bit mysterious to the average man. Guys are not always good at reading a woman's mind or understanding what's really going on in her life.
Here's a fresh view of a modern-day woman. In addition to being informative, hopefully this will also remove some of the preconceptions or myths that have polluted the dating world. At the end of the day, when two people want a genuine relationship, the steps are not that complicated. All it takes is a little bit of practice, a little bit of creativity, a little bit of inspiration and a little bit of bravery.

The last thing you want, as a man, is to be discarded into the "average" category by a woman who you're dating or interested in dating. When this happens, you can get stuck in a vicious cycle of dating women who, in the end, are not all that interested in you. If you want to be successful in dating, it is paramount to build your own personality and to know who YOU are. You will need to establish a set of behaviors that are yours and of which you are proud of. These behaviors need to include a mixture of some solid traditional values as well as other strong unique character actions.

Let's backtrack for a moment. Why am I writing this guide? Well, being a woman and having been in the dating world for a long time, I've experienced nearly every behavior men have to offer. Some were definitely good…other ones not so much.

I've been interested and passionate about this field for a very long time. Out of this passion was born my dating and singles website: StellaSingles.com. It's a community where singles can date, mingle, as well as ask questions and get answers from fellow members including myself. It's a place that feels like "home" for singles, which is something I felt was lacking online.

Since becoming a Certified Dating Coach and a Law of Attraction Coach, I've been guiding my clients in their lives and helping them build healthy successful relationships. I help singles with their online dating profile, dating questions, as well as more elaborate dating coaching.

In addition, having lived in different countries, I have a unique perspective on what drives men and women to date, love, and have relationships. I have seen what works and what doesn't. In this book, I'm ready to share it all with you.

Please note that some of these concepts may appear to you as just "normal" stuff. If you feel this way, great! That means you're already doing the right things. It may surprise you but often women are not looking for over-the-top displays of affection from a man. In today's dating world, normalcy is actually quite rare. As they say: "All the good ones are taken."

So again, while you may think that some of the advice in this book is "normal", the reason why I'm pointing it out is because many men miss those steps. For whatever reason, men often skip over the simplest and most straightforward elements in dating. Or, they don't realize the value of certain steps.

That's why, as a man, it's so important to place yourself in a woman's shoes from time to time. That's the only way you'll be able to fulfill her needs and stand out as that special guy.

As noted above, many of those things are easy, little things. However, it's the little things that often count more than the big ones. Why? Because it shows you care.

In this guide, I'll be focusing on everyday tips. These behaviors will place you a level ahead of the everyday, 'average' guy, putting you in prime position to begin and maintain a healthy long-lasting relationship with a great girl.

When reading these tips, please be advised that you don't have to do them ALL. The last thing I want is for you to feel you must become a "slave" to a woman in order for her to like or love you. On the contrary, none of these tips will make you a slave. Instead, you will be doing the things that so many other men don't. There are too many weird, awkward or otherwise defective guys out there. If you don't want to be one of them, then follow this advice. By doing these "normal" things, you will stand out…I can assure you.

To make things easier, I have presented you with a list that will help position yourself as a strong man in the eyes of your woman and will help you succeed in your dating endeavors.

First, I will go into the personality traits that you need in order to be the right guy for your girl. These are very important. Don't, however, feel that any of these tips demand that you change the way you are. You should always be yourself, but you must keep in mind that compromise is the key to success. Women will be looking for these traits when dating a guy. Don't underestimate the power of these personality traits.

After the personality overview, I will discuss which emotional triggers are important to connect with a woman. These are paramount in building the man-woman bond. This will help you look very attractive in the eyes of a woman and will put the chances on your side. Most women can't resist a man who can create the chemistry and special moments to remember forever. So pay extra attention.

Next, I will continue by listing actions that men can perform to please their woman, putting all of the luck on their side. Since men are action-oriented, this shouldn't be that hard to do. So, keep these in mind and make the moves when appropriate.

Finally, we'll wrap up with some thoughts on why it sometimes seems so complicated to date women. We'll debunk some myths and help you see what the differences are between a good guy and a not-so-good guy.

Once you've mastered these elements, you will feel more self-confident and more confident with women. And that's what women like! The contents of this book will not only protect you from being the "bad one that's left", but help you become the "good one that's taken."

Without further ado, let's get started.

Enjoy and have fun!

- Stella

CHAPTER 1. PERSONALITY TRAITS

1. Self Confidence, Not Arrogance

The number one rule is to be confident. A lot of men confuse this with being arrogant. There is a huge difference between the two in the eyes of a woman.

A confident man takes the lead, but is flexible with his woman. He's a gentleman, yet knows what he wants. He takes charge of a situation, but is not domineering or imposing. His behavior is classy and subdued, yet strong. He has thick skin for challenges in life, but handles them smoothly. He's sensitive to his woman's needs. Being confident really comes from the inside of who you are. It's the internal power that you feel. When that's the case, you don't need to externalize less-attractive behaviors in order to seem confident.

An arrogant man is full of himself, talks more about himself than anything else, isn't interested or sensitive to the woman he's dating, doesn't care to make an effort for her and clearly is just out for himself and his pleasures.

Men often assume that women just want a confident guy. So, they think that being loud and obnoxious to a waiter or cutting in front of a crowd will score him some points. Unfortunately, a serious woman will see through this behavior very quickly.

If you want to show confidence, it's a much more subtle skill. It really comes down to being confident in your good nature and your good intentions. It is treating people with respect. It is standing your ground in critical situations when you know you're right, without being rude. It is being a gentleman without feeling that you're a doormat. It is being proud of your achievements without throwing them in the face of every woman you meet. It is not using manipulation to get what you want.

Simply put, it comes down to being humble and strong.

2. Leadership, Not Control

Similarly, when it comes down to being a leader, women love men who can take charge. This goes hand-in-hand with being confident. It helps women feel secure and know that their man knows his way in the world and can defend her and potentially their home and family in the future. It's a very basic, instinctual need in women and it goes a long way.

That is not to say that it always needs to be in a major area, such as being a leader in your job or having your own business. Even if you have a regular job or no job at all, being a leader can just mean taking charge. For example, when entering a restaurant, you talk to the hostess and ask for a table. You also walk ahead of your date when the waitress is leading you to your table. You are leading your lady. Even in the most traditional etiquette books, a man leads the way to a table in a restaurant.

Here's a common scene: A female takes a guy with her to a car dealership so that he can help her negotiate a good deal. Yet, when they arrive, he just sits silently next to her while she does all the talking. This is a major turnoff and you can bet that the woman will be disappointed. Don't speak beyond your own knowledge base, but be assertive and strong nonetheless. Do a little research of your own perhaps, so you have some idea of what you're talking about.

So guys, be aware of the typical areas where men are expected to take charge and lead! This will go a long, long way with your lady.

Keep in mind this is very different from being controlling. When you lead, you make suggestions for a date, but leave the final decision up to them. For the first three dates you should plan what the two of you will do, but remain flexible for any conflicts with her schedule or preferences. After that, you can lead by proposing and she can pick something she likes.

If you're a control freak, then you will tend to insist on only doing what you want, when you want. You will want it your way and will feel threatened and insecure if the woman is unhappy with your plans. It's very important to catch yourself when you do that, as this will quickly lead to you manipulating the situation or starting to play games, which as we know is a big no-no on the road to success with women!

So keep in mind the distinction. When you're starting to feel threatened or insecure or, worse, controlled, ask yourself why this is happening. Most likely it is because your status quo, or your ego, feels threatened. Remember that that's a false signal. Don't fall into that trap or you may lose a great girl due to your own issues.

3. Be Funny and Witty

Women love men who make them smile and laugh. If you're funny, you could be a great date and attract many women. Too many guys these days are too serious. That is boring for women. They want someone who is witty and exudes self-confidence. They want a sense of humor.

That doesn't mean you should crack stupid jokes all the time, or worse, only talk in humorous or sarcastic tones. This will quickly make you look like a nut. This is especially popular on online dating profiles. It's a sure way to scare women off.

Instead of too much or too little, witty humor is something that you sprinkle around, here and there. You can be goofy sometimes as well. It's all a matter of measure. One thing is sure: not enough guys are appropriately humorous and if you put yourself out there and are funny, women will love you.

Why is it so important? Well, women like a man who doesn't just think in linear terms. Too many men are like that. They have their jobs and they approach life in the same way as their work. That's wrong. Dating doesn't work like that. When a man can laugh at himself or at a situation he is in, that means he can think outside of the box. It also sends a subtle message to the woman that if she were to talk about a sensitive subject, he actually may be open enough to "get" it, since his brain works in a multi-dimensional way.

4. Know What You Want

Be a man who knows what he wants. I cannot stress this enough. Confidence and leadership go hand-in-hand, and a man who knows what he wants will have both.

This means no wishy-washy projects or opinions on what your goals are for the future. A man who is confident definitely will project the image of a man who knows what he wants. You need to show determination, motivation and enthusiasm for things that are going on in your life, whether it's your job, your family, the place where you live, the trip you'd like to take or even the job search strategies you plan to apply to find your dream job.

It doesn't need to be grandiose: you don't need to say that you plan on building a hotel in order to sound like you have "big plans". It can be very simple. You need to show your girl that you have plans for your life, such as applying for a new job or proudly achieving that project your boss gave you.

You don't need to make big, life changing statements to prove that you know what you want. You can just mix it into the conversation. You may have a desire to get a pet or to pick up a hobby or to start fixing up your home/apartment. All these things may not be that big, but they show a determination and energy in your character, and that's what's important.

5. Call, Call, Call (or Consistency)

Does this sound scary? Are you thinking of the three-day rule – waiting three days before calling after the first date? Are you concerned about being viewed as overly pushy? Or too interested? Or, are you afraid of being rejected?

We women understand that all this may be going through your head, but remember – it is all in YOUR head! It is negative thinking, based on fear, insecurities or even selfishness. You don't need to give into that!

It is very important, as a guy, to understand that if you don't call, you're saying that you are not interested. That's all! There is nothing more to it. You are just plain not interested! Do you really want the woman of your dreams to think that you're not interested?

Also, remember that women still have that traditional role in society to sit and wait for a call. Not only is it nerve-wracking to wonder if the guy you just so greatly connected with will call, but it is also something that ends up losing the momentum if you don't follow up on time.

Maybe you never thought of it this way, but the momentum in a relationship, especially in the early stages, is very important! Women have a strong sensitivity to it, so don't blow it. Life is too short. If you met a woman and you enjoyed talking with her and can envision dating her, call or email her sooner rather than later. It will pay off in the end. You will both get to enjoy the momentum that has built up when you two meet again.

So, in practical terms, if you've had a first encounter, it's OK to call the next day. When I say "call, call, call," I obviously don't mean you should be calling her two or three times in a day – let alone more than that.

What I mean is that you need to come through and be consistent. This shows that you are someone she can rely on, that you have integrity and that you are interested. Again, this speaks to a woman's primal instinct of feeling protected and being able to rely on a man. Very important!

And if you don't think your connection with her is going anywhere, call and tell her so. She'll be more than happy to finally get an honest guy and will respect you even more, even if you are no longer dating. That's a lot of good karma!

6. Be a Gentleman

This may sound cliché, but girls love it when guys open car doors, carry their bags or suitcases, ask them if the temperature in the car is to their liking etc.

Again, with women, little things go a long way. Don't get sloppy or lazy, as these are the things that will differentiate you from other men.

You may think that with the "emancipation" of the sexes, there is more equality so women don't expect it. You would be wrong! Women like to be romanced in many different ways.

Guys need to put themselves in women's shoes. Never underestimate the value of nice gestures. To show a woman you care, you need to constantly be creative, respectful, romantic etc. Again, we're not saying it needs to be over-the-top all the time, but you need to show her you care.

I'll list some more things later on that gentlemen can do, but the basics are: good manners, pick her up, walk her to her car, bring her flowers, hold her hand when rollerblading, give her compliments on her hair or clothing. You get the idea.

Courting is a long-lost art. Don't be the guy who thinks it's not that important. It is important! Remember, women relate differently than men do. What may not be important for guys can be very important for women and vice versa.

7. Be Honest

The art of honesty is almost entirely lost in our society, yet it's really easy! It takes less energy to be honest than to lie. Honesty means you're strong enough to tell the truth. If you're going in zigzags, you're not honest.

The whole idea that by hiding the truth you'll be saving the other person from being hurt is totally false. It sounds like something that men made up to rationalize not having to come forward with explanations and feelings.

It's imperative to know that women would much rather have a guy call or email and say "Sorry, I enjoyed meeting you but I just don't feel the chemistry is there," than to have to wait and wonder why they haven't called or made plans.

Guys, please understand that it's really hard to be on the receiving end of "having to wait for a call." I'm sure if you put yourselves in a girl's shoes, you would hate this idea too, especially considering men are action and result-driven. So, it is easy to see how having to wait without knowing might drive someone crazy pretty quickly.

Please do women a favor and explain yourselves when something is wrong or off. You'd be surprised how responsive and understanding most women would be to that. Remember, you can still remain friends even if you're breaking it off.

Honesty is important in all aspects of life. If you're running late, it's very easy to text and say why. If you have something going on and can't get together, then explain why, don't hide behind excuses.

A whole book can be written on the subject on how to communicate honestly. Again, it's much easier than you think. Both of you will be relieved once you know where you stand – no matter what the subject is.

So be that guy, stand out from others and choose the path of honesty and integrity. It will pay you back 1000-fold.

8. Fight Your Ego

Dealing with ego is a tricky thing. Lots of men believe that they need to give into their egos, as it directly equates to their male pride. Some women even use the male ego to their advantage, inflating it until they get what they want.

However, ego is your number one enemy, no matter if you are a man or a woman. Women have learned to have a better handle on it over the years, but guys are still often enslaved to it.

Why is it bad? Because it makes you stubborn and a prisoner to beliefs and desires that in the long run go against what's best for you and any potential relationship you wish to have. When you listen or give in to your ego, you're not free (contrary to what many may believe). It's paramount to look at your actions or words and analyze them, preferably beforehand, to determine if they are driven by ego or a higher purpose.

Ego often kicks in when fear is involved. Fear of rejection, fear of losing control, fear of the unknown.

You need to be able to acknowledge that feeling of fear so that you can get past it. It's only when you realize how enslaved you are to the ego that you will be able to break free.

For example, you may be afraid of losing control and as a result you decide when and how you see your date. If she can't make it for whatever reason, you immediately take it personally and feel out of control. You try to impose your views on her or you try to 'retaliate' by not scheduling anything else for a long time. In this situation, your ego is leading you down the wrong path. This may be a great girl, but you're enslaved to your feelings of fear of losing control. Don't do it. When you meet someone you like, don't let your ego dictate the relationship. Women see though that anyway and may even respond with a counter-attack of ego-stroking and manipulation. It can become a vicious circle of manipulating games. You both will be losers in this game. Instead you could be winners.

So, try to see when you behave out of your ego or when it's genuine. Snap out of ego states and enjoy the road.

9. Be Generous

Too many men are concerned with the idea of "gold diggers." This is a widely misunderstood and misused concept and it's easy to hide behind it.

When dating, it's imperative to be generous. Maybe you already are a very generous guy or maybe you tend to be more on the tightfisted side of the equation. Don't be stingy. You need to be generous, very generous!

I cannot stress this enough. Do away with thoughts of being used. That's something that guys hide behind when they are insecure.

Today still, men tend to make more money and have easier advancements in their careers. That fact alone should make you proud about being able to treat and spoil your girl.

Aside from the materialistic considerations, it's in women's psyche to be with a man that will take care of her. I can already sense your feelings of unease. But wait, "taking care" doesn't mean that you need to be married tomorrow. What it means is that you are a proud man of who you are and what you have. By being generous, you are sending signals to the woman that she can rely on you, that you are responsible and giving and that you are not a user. Isn't it a great feeling to have? For women, it will give a feeling of security – a very strong feeling that guys shouldn't underestimate. If you can provide her with such a feeling, you're already halfway there.

So, what does it mean to be generous? Well, you can pay for her dinners, don't ever ask if she can pay, buy her a little something if you're out and about, bring her flowers, buy food when you're cooking together, take her on a trip. This will get you far!

How to tell if she's using you? If she "never" contributes to anything, if she keeps asking for things despite your generosity or if you paying for dinner ever becomes "expected", then watch out. There certainly is a fine line between being very generous and being used. You just need to listen to your gut on how the relationship is going and if she's a grateful girl.

Put the fears aside and enjoy the reputation of being a generous man. Here's a little secret: There is a saying that goes around amongst women: "When a guy is generous with money, he's generous in bed", aka is a good lover. Isn't that the reputation you'd like to have?

10. Be A Good Listener

Women are different from men. When you're interested in dating a woman, you need to put yourself in her shoes. While you may want to process a problem internally and then come up with a solution, women often know the solution already or aren't even seeking one to begin with. It's important for women to vent and to know that someone else is paying attention - actively listening - to what they are saying.

So, if your girl is complaining to you about her day or her friends or anything, really, she may just be venting. Don't interrupt her every two seconds with an idea of how to fix things, just let her speak! Don't dismiss what she's saying as unimportant or trivial and don't be judgmental! I repeat, do not dismiss or judge! Even if it's negative or sad, let her finish.

Once a woman has vented, she'll feel lighter and will be thankful for your patience. Only give her advice or a fix if she asks for it. Otherwise, you may be better off just saying "Yeah, that must be hard" or "You must feel exhausted" or "That must have been painful." Notice how you're acknowledging her feelings as opposed to giving her advice on how to solve the problem. Ask her questions. This is one of the most important things to remember if you ever wish to understand women.

11. Be Compassionate

This is similar to being a good listener. You need to be able to empathize with your girl's issues, problems or challenges. Don't dismiss them but instead, patiently try to put yourself in their shoes. How would you feel if this happened to you?

Give her a hug or cuddle up when she's sad or worried. Touch is very important so don't underestimate the power of physical contact.

Do something for her to help her out in a difficult moment. If she's sick, call to check up on her, bring her groceries, cook a meal for her, drive her to her doctor's appointment.
If she just bombed a job interview, discuss possible solutions for the next one, give her a big hug and tell her that you're confident that eventually she will succeed.

12. Be Social

You may be a shy guy or perhaps you feel uncomfortable in new situations. Well, if a woman you like is introducing you to her friends or family, you need to make an extra effort to blend in and be social. Don't sit by yourself with a blank face. Even if her friends are not your cup of tea, make an effort to have some small talk, to ask questions or at least pretend to laugh.

One of the fastest ways to show a woman you're not compatible with her is to be "out of touch" when in social situations. If you're showing an absent face and sitting in the corner, it will become clear right away that you're not a good fit. Above that, her friends may make negative comments about you later-on if you appear uninterested or unwilling to be social with them.

So, even if you're not totally comfortable, please go out of your way to be friendly and social.
As a relationship grows you can revisit the friend situation and possibly mention that you don't think they are a good fit for you or for her. In the early dating days though, that's not the route to take.

So, try to be social. Even if you're normally shy.

13. Respect Women

Men don't like it when women bash men. It makes them feel deficient and uncomfortable. The same is also true the other way around.

You may like the girl you're dating but if you're constantly complaining about how women are in general, she may start to think that you feel that way about her as well. So, don't say that women are bitchy, catty, jealous or gold diggers. This really will only show that you have a complex towards women.

Women like a man who likes and respects women. It doesn't mean that you're a player. It means that you respect women for who they are.

Note: men of older generations sometimes have more sexist views towards women than the newer generations. Younger men often find it normal to have a woman boss or to be with a smarter woman than themselves. So, if you're easily influenced by those old-fashioned views, it may be time to drop them and be part of the newer trends.

14. Don't Constantly Talk About Yourself

It's normal to be nervous on a date. Some people talk more, others less when they're under stress. However, try to keep it under control. Don't talk about yourself all the time. It will look as if you're very self-centered. And women don't want to be with a self-centered guy, who only cares about himself and his adventures.

So, ask your date questions about her life or simply talk about common subjects so that both of you can participate. It will make for a fun and light-hearted conversation, without putting either one of you on the spot. When each person can share something about themselves and talk about current events, a stronger connection is usually the result.

15. Dress Nice and Be Clean

As a single guy, you may be used to being casual and relaxed. Maybe you don't always shave, or clean your apartment, for example. You'd be surprised how bad an impression you would make if your place weren't tidy. If you're inviting a date to your place, go out of the way to organize things, clean everything up and show your place in the best-possible light.

Keep your bathroom and bathtub clean! Clean your toilet. When a guy shows he's not too sanitary and messy, it can really disgust a woman and you could lose her just based on that. Women tend to have a higher standard of cleanliness, so the more you do, the better.

When you're getting ready for a date, dress nicely. Avoid wearing sandals that show your toes unless you are going somewhere outdoors in the summer. Men's toes aren't the most attractive and many women would much rather see a guy that is wearing closed shoes.

Wear a nice shirt. Make sure it's clean and you can even put on some cologne. The point is, it's better to be overdressed than underdressed when you're with a woman.
It's hard to erase a bad first impression, so make sure you're clean.

But…

16. Don't be a Clean Freak

Now that we have established that men need to make sure they're neat and clean, it's important to talk about a type of man that most women will not want to meet: the neat freak.
Those guys seem to apply their zest for perfection in every part of their lives: work, play and love. It's certainly good to be neat, but when it becomes an obsession for things to be perfect, it sends a signal to women that you are a demanding person. When a man is

an obsessive-compulsive clean freak, women may begin to feel insecure.

So pay attention: are you obsessed with everything needing to be perfect? Are you applying this to the women in your life? If so, you may be a bachelor set in his ways that most women will be afraid to date. If you are and you still want to date quality women, loosen up, don't sweat the small stuff. Life is too short for perfection and no one is perfect.

CHAPTER 2. EMOTIONAL TRIGGERS

Women are emotional creatures. They are sensitive and loving. You can make a woman feel special by opening those channels and connecting with her on that level. When a woman feels special, she'll be very connected to you. It is said that we make people fall in love with us based on how we make them feel. So if you can make a woman feel deep, loving emotions, you're well on your way to capturing her heart.

It's really not that hard to do. Guys tend to overthink this. All you need to do is be lighthearted, friendly, romantic and open to create and build special feelings between the two of you.

The reverse is also true. When men stop "working at it," then the chemistry and the connection quickly disappear. This is why people say that relationships take work. It's not just work from a practical point of view. Rather, it's keeping the connection alive and of course both parties need to work at it. But, since this guide talks about what men can do to be forever attractive to women, we're focusing on that. Women are like flowers. You need to water them and provide them with sunshine regularly. Otherwise, they will hang their heads and wilt.

17. Create Magic

Life is not easy for anyone. Responsibilities, stress, financial burdens, family obligations – you name it – tend to creep up in our daily lives and we forget to create magic.

It's important to remember that there is something amazing about every day you live. Be grateful for what you have and who you meet. Try to see the good in every situation and every person.

When it comes down to dating and impressing women, if you know how to create magic moments, you will instantly enhance the chemistry and connection between the two of you. I define magic as saying or doing things that are out of the ordinary. They don't need to be over-the-top type of gestures. Instead, what I'm talking about are emotional moments that create unforgettable memories.

This kind of behavior requires a little bit of spontaneity and a little bit of risk-taking, but the rewards are exponential. When you create magical moments, you energize everything in the body and the brain of both people. It's like a serotonin high. This is what bonds and connects two people. You would be surprised how easy it is to do and how powerful it is.

Let me give you some examples:

- Let's say you had a first date and you think you enjoyed each other. Instead of doing the same old thing of going for drinks after the dinner you just had, you take your girl for a walk on the beach. Both of you are completely in awe of the waves splashing on the sand, the moon reflecting in the water and the smell and the sound of sea water. This is magic. You don't even need to talk. You can just embrace each other or admire the scenery in silence. Hold her hand and don't say anything. Or give her a very gentle kiss and then keep walking. Or you could be silly and splash and run through the waves (if the water is warm enough). The options are endless and these moments will be unforgettable for both of you.
- Instead of creating a classic date, take her on a tour of something new and interesting. You can give her a tour of a winery you like. Show her a new hole-in-the-wall restaurant. Take a drive through a beautiful scenery or tour a special neighborhood. Show her a historical landmark and tell her some background on it on the way to or from your date. Stop the car and grab her hand and look her in the eyes. Be romantic. Exchange that special energy that is created between two human beings. It's much more powerful than anything you would say or do. It's something you don't see, but you definitely feel it. Don't make it sexual, make it romantic and gentle.

- Create a surprise moment if you know what kind of music she likes. Get that CD and play it in your car while you're driving to the date. As you talk about it, look deeply into her eyes. Try to find that connection. This is when magic happens. If it feels right, kiss her gently, very gently. Again, don't make it a sexual thing, just kiss and keep going.

I hope you get the picture by now. The sky is the limit when it comes down to creating those special moments. And you'll be a man in control and will create a lot of charisma for yourself if you just keep it light and non-sexual. Kiss her slightly and then move on. Look deeply in her eyes. Touch her hands or her shoulder or her back and keep going. It's those little moments that really solidify a connection. It turns women on like you can't believe. This is what builds chemistry and what shows you really care and are interested.

18. Be Passionate

In this capitalistic society that focuses on shallow values, people have almost forgotten how to be passionate. I am not talking about being passionate about your car, your hobbies, your job or other materialistic goodies. I am also not referring to passion in a sexual sense.

Passion is much larger than that. It's passion for life and passion for love. It's a passion for living at the highest emotional level you can and creating the best connection possible with a special woman. This is a more subtle skill than just "jumping" on someone with French kisses or other sexual advances. The real passion is the passion of the soul, of how you are toward that person you are passionate about.

It's kissing with your emotions coming through. It's being in touch with yourself and knowing what you have to offer the woman you like. It's stroking her hair and enjoying the smell of it, like flowers. It's touching her cheek and feeling a tingling when you do it. It's being sensitive to the other person and embracing the moment.

Try to be a passionate man. Be passionate about the love you'd like to create and the life you'd like to live. Feel comfortable in your skin and know that there are a lot of special moments that can be created between two human beings. Don't just go through the motions in a routine way. Put your feeling into it. This is, again, what will create a special connection. If you touch her hand, do it with feeling. If you look her in the eyes, look deeply and sincerely.

There is a French song that goes something like this: "And we made love just with our eyes." Keep this in mind. This transcends rough sexuality and seduction. It's a more subtle, but incredibly powerful tool.

19. Out Of Control

Another thing that makes people fall in love is when they feel the person they like is just slightly out of reach. It's this feeling of being "out of control" that creates special sensations in someone.

Have you noticed that when someone is too available and too easy to reach, you lose some of the chemistry? Of course you have. You're a man and you like the chase. However, this is not so much about the chase as it is about leading the relationship and being in control as you the man. This is not the same as being controlling. No. It's about creating an environment where everything builds up for the both of you.

If you leave the girl just slightly "out of control," then she's much more likely to fall for you. This does not mean: not calling back, disappearing, being unpredictable or being a jerk. The subtle out-of-control feeling that the woman will get is when you take the lead, then here and there you sprinkle it with a surprise or spontaneity. Make it so that there is always more to find out about who you are. Make sure to be a nice guy, not a game player, but at the same time be interesting and creative. Don't lay it all out there. Keep a little bit of a secret here and there so her curiosity will be triggered. You will stand out as an out-of-the-ordinary man.

20. Vulnerability

In our macho society, men are groomed to be strong and unemotional. However, if you want to be successful with women, it's also important to show your "weaker" side here and there. You know why? It's been scientifically proven that people often fall for a perceived weak spot in someone. This doesn't mean that you shouldn't be a strong man. On the contrary: a strong man knows himself and his vulnerabilities and is not afraid to show them. It's only when you're insecure that you try to cover up some of your vulnerabilities or weaknesses. When men are overconfident, it often also means that they are covering up insecurities. Sometimes, a more reserved man, who holds himself confidently but doesn't talk so much, actually appears to be more of a quality man. A man who can mention a vulnerability he has and not be ashamed of it shows a great deal of strength.

It becomes an endearing quality for the woman and she will feel a much deeper connection to you when you also show a little bit of your vulnerable side.

What does vulnerability exactly entail?

- The fact that you were hurt in your prior relationship (but you're over it now).
- The fact that you can sometimes be shy.

- Expressing some of your feelings and/or emotions about the woman you're dating makes you more vulnerable, but oh so much more endearing.
- If you are afraid of heights (or anything else), you can mention that.
- If you cry when you watch sad movies, that's an incredible emotional trigger for a woman. This means you are a sensitive man who is not afraid of his emotions.
- If you're tired of the politics in your work place and you mention it to your date, it means you acknowledge the harsh reality of working in the corporate world (but don't whine about this or constantly complain about your job).
- You miss your family or your kids when they are gone.

21. Charm/Gallantry

Be a charming and chivalrous man. This is not just reflected in actions, but in your overall behavior. It really encompasses several of the points mentioned in Chapter 1 and Chapter 3.

Bring the lady home and wait until she's inside before you drive off. Open doors for her. Walk on the right side of the street (on the road side, which means that she's protected from potential oncoming cars). Pour her drink first. Give her the best seat in the theatre, the best dish or the best spot when watching an event. Being elegant and respectful will make you stand out. Don't be sloppy about things. Put some thought into it. Act with awareness. Don't just do things robotically, but put some thought in everything you do and say. Be an aware man.

22. Physical Touch

Physical touch is really important. Again, it's like tending to a garden. Women are very sensitive to physical touch, but it needs to be done right. No brusque gestures, aggressive kisses or rough touches. It needs to be gentle and sensual, without being sexual. You need to put your passion, as well as respect for the woman, into any kind of physical contact you make with her. Respect means no vulgar or overly sexual gestures. Instead, focus on being romantic. When a man is romantic, it makes a woman dream. It sends her to seventh heaven.

Physical contact includes:

- Touching her hand, shoulder, elbow or lower back. Do it very briefly and gently. Just enough to send through that beam of energy through her body.
- Kissing. Gentle, passionate and sensual is the best way. Don't overdo the manly thing anddon't be overbearing. But also don't be so gentle that not enough energy flows. Kissing is really an art and very few men actually know how to kiss a woman.

Yet, it's one of the most powerful, if not the most powerful, ways of making a woman yours.

- Holding hands. Do it spontaneously and not constantly. Just enough to trigger her interest and curiosity, but remain in control whether you are holding her hands or not.
- Cuddling. This is a great way to build closeness with the person. It doesn't need to go any further than that. Don't take it to the next level of being intimate. Stop it just in time. It will show that you are confident and in control and I can guarantee you she will want more. But keep that suspense just for a little while. It's all about building anticipation!
- Whispering into her ear. This is a very sexy thing to do. You need to find the right moment for this, but whispering in a woman's ear is sure to build more attraction. Keep it short and don't say anything sexual. Instead, focus on either a random fact or a complement to. Beware of saying something cheesy or trying too hard. It needs to be spontaneous and light. Be charming when doing that.

23. Decisiveness

If you've paid attention to my tips, you may have noticed a common thread to the message and that is being decisive. It shows you know what you want and are a leader.

Learn to make good decisions quickly. It's a sexy quality to a man. If you're going to dinner and they've lost your reservation, be decisive and propose a great alternative. If the sky is clear and the stars are bright, propose an evening walk along the river. If a street is blocked off, be decisive about going a different route to get to your destination.

A confident man is decisive, not wishy-washy. Your mind is quick and sharp and you know what to do in any given situation. This will certainly add to your sex appeal. Women love a man who can decide. This doesn't mean being controlling and imposing. Rather, it means being decisive on the spot, when something unforeseen happens.

CHAPTER 3. ACTIONS THAT WILL GET YOU NOTICED

24. Open Doors

Perhaps you consider yourself to be a casual, modern guy and don't necessarily live by traditional gender rules. However, the fact remains: women still love it when guys open doors for them. It's a simple gesture but it means you care. Why not score some brownie points by doing this simple act?

Don't just go and unlock the car door, actually go and open it for her too. Open the doors to restaurants and buildings as well. She'll notice your good manners and your classy behavior. That's hard to come by these days.

25. Bring Flowers

Oh how you will stand out if you bring her flowers! First date, second date, tenth date – it doesn't matter. Women love flowers.

Or, you could be a special and creative guy and bring just one flower each time you see her. That will get you noticed and she'll love you for that.

26. Send Little Gifts

This doesn't mean you have to constantly give her things. What this means is that once in a while, you can show her you care by bringing her a little something special. Or, if you went on a trip, you can bring a little souvenir. Or maybe you saw something online and printed it out for her. The list is endless but those little gestures will score you points, so don't disregard them.

27. Say "Thank You"/Texting

After the first date, text or email to say thank you and make a point to mention how much you enjoyed your time together. It's very simple, it takes three seconds and it will go a long way.

It shows you are interested – of course. It also shows you have manners, you don't play games and you don't take your time with her for granted.

If you're running late, text her so she knows. You can also text her to tell her you're on your way.

DON'T sit and text while you're with your date though. That's impolite and you will lose points for rudeness. As a matter of fact, put your phone on silent so that she can see how important she is to you.

You don't need to text after each date, just here and there. Definitely after the first date! She will see you as a caring man and will be excited even more to see you the next time.

After this message, don't wait forever to set the next date. Do it within the next couple of days. Set the date for a day that's out at least three days. This again will show that you are polite and respectful of her time, and that you like planning ahead. All these are ingredients for a genuine connection.

Don't be afraid that this is setting you up immediately for a serious relationship. Don't feel trapped. It is just a way to demonstrate your strengths as a man. You'll be viewed as a confident leader who knows what he wants. These are the top 3 qualities women are looking for!

28. Say "Hi"

Women like continuity. If you don't have plans for another date for longer than a few days, call to say "hi." Show interest. Don't just call because you need to make plans.

Ask her questions about her day and talk about your day. Let her vent about something that happened without judging or interrupting. Listen! Don't be impatient. Be genuinely interested in her, her life, her job, her pets, her family, her friends, etc.

Don't go off a check list of questions. Be natural in your conversation. Be fluid and light. Be fun!
Don't keep her on the phone for too long. Once you've shared some stories, wish her a good night and tell her you'll call her later to make plans or to pick her up etc.

29. Pick Her Up

No matter how far you live from each other, pick her up. This is not to say that you need to always do it no matter how long you've been together, but when you start out dating someone, please make that effort.

If you met online however, then it's fair for each of you to drive and to meet at a neutral location. After a couple of dates, when both of you are more comfortable, ask her if you can pick her up. If she still wishes to drive separately, then that means it's still too early, but that doesn't necessarily mean she doesn't like you. Going, literally, that extra mile will show that you are interested and that you are not a lazy person. It means you are willing to work for what you desire. And that's a highly sought-after quality.

30. Be a Handyman

Did you know that women LOVE handy guys? Some men will put on their online dating profiles that they have the money to pay someone else to fix things in their house. Well, that's actually a bit of a turnoff for women. Why? Because it comes off as not handy and at the same time a bit arrogant. That may not have been the intent, but that's how women will see things. It's better not to put that in your profile at all.

So, yes, women like guys who know how to use their hands. Just like men may appreciate women who cook, women like guys that can fix things in the house, in the car, in the yard. You can get a lot of brownie points for helping her with some problem in the house if you hear her mentioning it. Just volunteer to help her out with something and your rating will raise instantly. Don't underestimate the power of being handy. The reason why it's a sexy quality for a woman is that it subconsciously also sends the message that you would be "handy" in other areas, if you catch my drift.

What if you're not handy? Well, first, don't advertise it openly. Second, see if you can still help her in some male-oriented department like helping her pick up stuff at Home Depot or mentioning some useful things about her A/C that is broken. Do some research online, print it out and show it to her. This will be almost as good as being handy. You will be helpful and that shows you're resourceful, no matter what the situation.

31. Be Creative

Creative doesn't mean being weird or "out there." Women like normalcy. Believe it or not, it's hard to meet guys that are normal. There are more weird men than normal left in the dating pool.

That's why being creative really means coming up with interesting activities, mixing it up, not settling into a routine.

What's Boring?

- A guy who always goes out to eat at the same 3 or 5 restaurants and is too lazy to try something new.
- A guy who always plans a movie night at home with takeout.
- A guy who doesn't have interests outside of his work.
- A guy who always says the same things, or uses the same sentences when texting or calling.

So guys, keep this in mind. Mix it up. You need to think outside the box and create fun times. Find new places to visit, museums to go to and outdoor concerts to attend. Mix it up with a home-cooked movie night at home, a hike with the dogs, a social event or even shopping together.

32. Surprise Her

Some women like surprises. Others don't. I would say the majority do. So, getting her a gift card for her favorite store and driving her over there as a surprise sounds like a great idea. Ordering a book that she's been talking about, taking her to an exhibit she's always wanted to attend, booking a weekend trip to a town she's been wanting to visit - these are all examples of fun and surprising things you can do. This kind of effort will go a long way.

How do you surprise her? Listen to what she says and talks about. If you're attentive, you'll know the things she longs to do. This will do a couple of things at the same time: it will prove that you are attentive to her and her needs, that you're a great listener, that you care about her and that you're creative. This will bring you closer and will make you appear much more valuable. So keep it up!

33. Show Her You Care About Her Pets

If she has dogs or cats, bring little gifts for them. Show them affection when you're coming over. Pet them, play with them, bond with them. If given the ultimatum, most women would sooner part with their boyfriends, than their loving pets. So, don't tease the animals or behave disrespectfully. That is a sure-fire way to get the boot.

34. Show Interest In Her Life

This could be as small as asking her how her day went. Or sending her an email about something she cares about.
It's the little things that count. The more attentive you are to the details of her life the more she'll appreciate you.
Saying something and doing something are two different things. Remember, actions speak louder than words.

35. Wish Her Goodnight and Sweet Dreams

Sending a quick text wishing her sweet dreams will be a nice bonus point. Don't make a super long conversation out of it. Just briefly show her you're thinking of her. It's very sweet when women get that from the guy. It gives a sense of security and sweetness.

Women like this kind of sweetness in a man. It's almost as if you're tucking her into bed - just through text.

36. Helping Without Expectation of Reciprocation

Offer to help in any way that you can, but don't place any conditions on it. It is a major mistake for men to think that if they do a favor for a woman, that they can then ask for something in return. Some guys subscribe to the notion that if they do something nice for their lady, they'll be thanked properly later on that evening, if you know what I mean.

This is a big no-no and a serious man who is interested in dating a woman he likes should NEVER do such a thing. If your lady asks you for help or advice, do NOT place any conditions on that. This not only creates awkwardness, but you'll destroy your reputation, let alone bring bad karma upon yourself by not being genuinely helpful. This is not what a generous man is like.

If a woman you like asks you for a favor, do it for her wholeheartedly and don't expect anything in return. She'll like you much more than if she felt pressured in returning the favor in whatever way you made it clear. Many women won't ever contact you again if that's what you're doing.

37. Emotions

Some men, especially when feeling defensive in an argument, will throw out the "don't be so emotional" defense. This is a very low blow! Men should never say such a thing, no matter the circumstance.

The fact is, women - and men, for that matter - are emotional. Emotions are part of being human. Love is an emotion, so is sadness and anger. The key is to work through negative emotions, and this means not denying or criticizing them.

When a man tells a woman she's too emotional, it's equivalent to emotional abuse. Men and women have feelings and they need to be acknowledged. By saying such a thing, a man immediately places blame on the woman and makes her feel guilty for who she is and what she feels. You wouldn't want a woman to attack who you are or how you feel, would you? So, never ever should men say these things to women. Instead, be constructive, open and compassionate in your conversation.

38. Embrace Her Hobby

What does the girl you date do for fun? What are her hobbies? Does she like hiking or playing tennis or painting or gardening?

Pay attention to her interests and once in a while get her a little gift or a surprise outing regarding her hobby. This will go a very long way. It's really not that hard to do, but it will send her a signal that you care and that you're interested and that you actually pay attention. It also shows it's not all about you. That's very important for most women, if not all.

So, if she likes painting sceneries and there is an exhibit at a local museum, take here there.
If tennis is her sport, make a point to watch her play or help her train.
If she likes gardening, compliment her on her garden or buy her a new plant. The list goes on and on. All it takes is paying a little bit of attention.

39. Bring Her To/From The Airport

I am not suggesting you need to become a doormat and do everything all the time, but women like help and enjoy someone who is sensitive to their needs. If she's taking a trip, ask her if she needs a ride. It's not a big deal, but it will save her on having to call a cab or a shuttle. Again, women enjoy being with a man who can help and take care of them. That's the main message. All you need to do is pay attention. This means get out of your shell and see how you can be helpful.

40. Help Her Draft Her Resume/Work Paper

This comes down to being helpful. If she has a need and is looking for a job or has a big project coming up for work, why not ask her if you can review or help her out with it. Not only will this be greatly appreciated, but also you'll spend time together in a serious endeavor, which is a nice way to get to know each other.

41. Use Romantic Words

Women love romance. It can be shown in many ways. One of the ways is to, once in a while, use romantic language. Beware though, don't start with it in the early days of dating and don't overdo it.

However, once you've been dating for one to three months, depending on how comfortable you are, you can call her honey or sweetie, or better yet, give her a unique and cute nickname. If you're apart, you can say you miss her.

When you use romantic language, it needs to be short. Don't say it every three seconds. Use it sparingly. It will have a stronger effect. If you overdo it, you may potentially chase her away. It needs to be appropriate and sincere, not just a space filler.

42. Cook Her Dinner

Not all men know how to cook, especially well. If you can cook though, share your talents with your date. Propose to cook for her. It will be fun and intimate, and she'll really appreciate it.

Since cooking is culturally considered a task for women, when a man cooks, women really do like it. It's a nice change and its fun. Plus, it expands both partners' horizons. Hopefully you can make something nice and healthy!

43. Play a Game

A great way to build closeness is to spend time together. There are hundreds of things you can do with someone and one of them is playing games. Whether it's a card game, a board game or an outdoor game, make it fun. Joke, laugh, be witty, be competitive but lighthearted. Never be a sore loser. It's fine to be competitive at work or the sports you're playing, but don't be competitive in the same way with the women you date.

Why? Because it's not something you're trying to win. The goal is to have fun and to build a nice connection; you're not competing for a promotion. You may say to yourself "I'm competing to be the best guy she ever met." While that's true, it is not something that gets achieved by winning by any means necessary. Put your ego aside and just have fun. If she wins, you'll score more points anyway.

44. Discuss Topics of Interest

A key ingredient in any relationship is communication. You should be able to talk about anything, whether it be intimacy, feelings, practical matters or what's going on in the world.
So, be an interesting guy: don't just talk about sports or things that relate to you. Show that you have an open mind and that you care about what's going on in the world around you.

You can talk about travel, interesting countries and cultures, the economy, nature, news, family, animals, museums, books, movies – the list is endless. The key is that you want to show that you're a curious guy, not just someone who only cares about football and beer.

45. Travel

If you've been dating for a month or longer, it's a great idea to book a daytrip somewhere. It doesn't need to be far away or expensive. Maybe on the outskirts of town there is a beautiful forest or river you would like to show her. Or there is an exhibit or wine tasting event that's a little further outside of town.

Just look up an event in your local paper or a local website and take her there. It's a great way to spend an active day together instead of always doing the same old stuff.

When you spend time together for more than 2 hours or so, you get to know each other much better. You bond and you really gain a better understanding of one another. There is less pressure as well.

So, mix it up a bit. Book a day trip and see how your relationship will blossom.

CHAPTER 4. WHY DATING CAN BE SO COMPLEX

Let me start by saying that dating doesn't have to be complex. We as humans make it so. However, there is hope. Every day, there are plenty of happy couples that form and go on to have successful and fulfilling relationships.

So, why do we make it so complicated on ourselves?
I believe that communication, not knowing what we want and not understanding the other person is what creates this cloud of confusion.
If you know what you want, whether it's a serious relationship of just casual dating, all you need to do is communicate that to your girl. You don't need to play games, lie or pretend to be something that you are not. Women really, really appreciate honesty. There aren't enough honest, straightforward guys out there.

When you play the honesty card, you'll get much better results. It will also give you more self-confidence in the fact that you are able to be who you are and to articulate your goals clearly.
Of course, there are plenty of women who have too much psychological baggage for this straightforward tactic to work every time. That's life though. Not everything fits into a pre-determined

mold. However, when you are looking to impress the right person for you, this is the right thing to do.

You need to strive for quality over quantity for yourself and for others. If you want quantity, it will come by being a person of quality.

As I mentioned before, trying to understand a woman from her point of view – putting yourself in her shoes – will get you much further in dating. Guys who are successful with women are those who know what women want. The difference between a player and a relationship-material guy is that the player is not sincere and has ulterior motives, while the serious guy is genuine! Remember, women are very intuitive and will pick up on it fast.

CHAPTER 5. MYTHS ABOUT WOMEN

There is much disinformation in our society pertaining to dating. That's why it's important to use your brain and to trust your gut.

While the detailed description about various myths would be the subject of a whole other book, I'd still like to briefly clarify why the personality traits and action points referenced above tend to result in successful dating.

- Women have basic desires – just like men. However, they are different from male desires. Society also puts a lot of limits and pressures on women and it's important for men to understand that.

- Women are not looking for men who play games and are generally uninterested in playing games themselves, despite what popular culture would have you believe.

- As women and men both evolve, communication and relationships will become more and more healthy and fulfilling. That's why you may need to throw out some of the preconceived ideas about women that you've been force-fed all your life by family, friends, colleagues or TV.

- Women still make less than men in the workplace. Career advancement is not as easy as it is for men. That's why it's so important for you to be generous and supportive of your girl. It's just a whole lot harder for women than for men to financially advance. That said, it doesn't mean that you need to become a doormat for a girl that doesn't care to do anything in her life. These kinds of women are, thankfully, becoming less and less common. You just need to be helpful and respectful and you'll be appreciated in turn.

- Even successful women need a man! This means that you still need to embrace some of the traditional roles while being open minded and supportive to the woman's life, her goals and her challenges. Yes, this means a little more work but it comes with greater benefits.

While some of your buddies may say that you need to focus on quantity rather than quality, in the long-term, it's a losing proposition. Why? Because while others evolve and grow in relationships, thereby polishing their skills for future encounters, you'll be left behind.

Experience and practice are key. You need to see what works for you and what doesn't. This is what will make you a good guy in the long run.

While being a player sounds appealing to many men, often they realize that there is no real substance to it – for themselves or for the women. It's much easier to say what your goals and intentions are up front and to have an honest relationship. It will be a win-win situation for both.

CONCLUSION

Well, that about wraps it up. I hope you were able to pull at least a few useful pieces of information from this guide. As I mentioned before, a successful relationship is the product of a number of different factors: practice, creativity, inspiration and, of course, bravery.

Observe what works best for you and what you struggle with. You can't expect to be the best at everything of course, so mix things up. Different women will have different needs and interests, requiring you to adjust your approach every time. Still, many of the familiar principal foundations will remain the same. In the end, trust your gut and you'll be okay.

At the core of every strong relationship is a high level of trust and honesty. This connection helps build the structure upon which the love between two people can grow. In today's world, we often forget what 'love' really is. With the endless list of everyday stresses that we encounter on a day-to-day basis, it can be easy to get distracted and disinterested. However, real connections are out there, I assure you, they just require a certain level of effort and time.

Don't get discouraged, the right person for you does exist – she is probably looking for you as you look for her. It would be a shame to miss out on such a wonderful connection, letting the opportunity of a lifetime slip right through your fingers. I encourage all singles to stop and think about what they really want. Review your goals and beliefs as they pertain to dating – and then compare that to the actions you normally take to attain them. If there is a disconnect between the two, perhaps you should consider making some changes in the way you approach the subject of love and dating.

When you become more aware of your own actions and how they may be perceived by others, you put yourself in a much greater position to succeed. Place yourself in someone else's shoes. See things from their end. Allow yourself time to reflect. As they say – "When your life story is written will you have any regrets?" Well, pretend you're 80, 90, 100 – how far have you come and what else do you wish to achieve? Not proud of your mistakes? Who is. If you acknowledge and forgive yourself though, you can move on. Pat yourself on the back for the great things you've done. We all have treasures in our hearts that are there for others to see. Be thankful for every little thing you have and try to build on that. When you're grateful, you feel great. And when you feel great, you can reach highs you've never reached before.

So, here's to you being a great man. Start today and you'll reap the benefits tomorrow!

Best,
From Stella, with kisses!

Please Leave A Review

If you enjoyed the book and found it helpful, please be so kind as to leave a review. This greatly helps with my books and with spreading the word for other men!

Made in the USA
Middletown, DE
11 September 2020